Under the Wings of Mister Dove

UNDER THE WINGS OF MISTER DOVE

Pastor J.L. Moore

ISBN: 0-75960-939-X

This book is printed on acid free paper.

1stBooks-rev. 1/24/01

CONTENTS

PREFACE

By the little doves trusting in the big white dove in the sky, they will be protected from all harm and evil. Nothing shall by no means hurt them.

Introduction

Mister Dove has wings that are as wide as the sky, his wings shield and protect the little doves that when it is raining, he is their shield. When the sun is beaming, shining brightly, his wings comfort them. Mister Dove likes to travel north, south, east and west. Therefore, he flies higher than any other bird in the air.

Mister Dove sits high in the sky, as if he holds the whole universe together. As Mister Dove sits, he likes to look over the whole earth. Watching all the people as they travel, coming and going. He likes to watch the children and see them smiling, and hear them laughing.

Mister Dove like to care for all the doves by flying in the direction of east where all doves may find nourishment, comfort, rest, and also where they may take shelter. East is Mister Dove's most favorable place. Therefore, he moves with the clouds.

As Mister Dove travels east the whole earth can be supplied and as he travels west, a little rain falls. When he travels upwards, a little snow falls, and as he rests, still much sunshine descends.

Chapter One

THE BLACK RAVEN

One day as Mister Dove was resting, he saw a black raven flying around the other doves and causing a big stir among the little doves. Mister Dove was very displeased and quickly he loosened one of his feathers and it landed on the Black Raven. The raven shouted, "forgive me," "forgive me," to the little doves and they forgave the raven. The raven turned into a dove and was joined together with the other doves under the wings of Mister Dove.

The Black Raven was stalking the other doves with his pointed beak causing them to beat against the other doves. The Black Raven was a naughty bird, he liked to cause trouble for the doves.

Chapter Two

THE HUGE WORM

One day as Mister Dove was resting, being very cautious as he saw the other doves singing and whistling seeking for food on the ground, there came creeping toward the doves this huge worm, too big for the doves to eat.

Then suddenly, a feather landed on the big worm from Mister Dove and the worm became smaller. It shrunk sizeable enough for the doves to eat. Therefore, they shared the worm and all were filled. They were filled because they shared the worm.

When you are able to help someone and do help them, you are left with a great smile and unspeakable joy. Every time Mister Dove descends a feather for good, he is replaced with another feather. By this, Mister Dove never gets bald.

Chapter Three

THE HEAVY RAIN AND MIGHTY WIND

As Mister Dove was resting, he felt the coming of a heavy rain and a rush of a mighty wind. The other doves were not aware of it. Therefore, they were singing and flocking together, busy playing until they heard a certain sound from mister Dove saying, "hunk, hunk," meaning, east, east.

They all with togetherness lifted up their wings and ascended into the air and headed east where they took shelter. East is their home and the place of Mrs. Dove. Mister Dove shields and protects the little doves and warns them of danger. The little doves don't always have to leave their play area.

Chapter Four

THE WANDERED DOVE

One day as the little doves were playing, one of the doves wandered off from the others deep into the woods. He was injured and was not able to return to the other doves. As time began to pass by and the sun was going down, the other doves began to get very concerned for the dove that wandered away.

The little dove that wondered off began to get very hungry and to be afraid. Then suddenly the other doves appeared to him and lifted the injured dove up and they all flew toward the east. There, Mrs. Dove began to take good care of the little dove that was injured.

As soon as the injured dove was cared for, they all began to eat, drink and be happy together because the wandered dove was returned with the others and made well. Mrs. Dove continued her job and Mister Dove continued seeing and hearing and the little doves continued to sing and flock together.

Chapter Five

THE HUGE ANT

The next day as the little doves were flying, they all at once landed on the grass and began to feed. As they were eating the friendly worms, there came crawling this huge ant. The ant was very hungry and had not eaten for days. He had a big appetite, so when he saw the doves eating, he said to himself, "yum, yum," meaning, food, food.

Therefore, he wanted to eat and his sight was not on the worm but on the doves. The huge ant crawled and crawled until he made his way to one of the doves and as he began to take a bite, Mister Dove said, "hunk, hunk," meaning, danger very near. All at once the little doves flew up and away together.

Chapter Six

NOISES IN THE NIGHT

Therefore, as the sun was setting and the brightness of the day began to come to an end. Mister Dove was resting in the sky. Therefore, he was so white until he glowed in the dark, his glow would give off a reflection of light until it would not be so dark when darkness came and the little doves would not be afraid.

Then all the little doves began to fall asleep and the reflection from Mister Dove shined on them as they were sleeping. Then suddenly there was a loud noise that sounded, bang! The little doves were awakened, amazed of what was happening. Mister Dove spoke, "hunk, hunk," to the doves, telling them to be not afraid.

Therefore, it was only the sound of cars moving in the night, animals creeping in the woods and people closing their doors. Then, the little doves began to ease and as they eased, they began to fall asleep again.

Chapter Seven

THE RIVER

On the early morning as the sun began to rise and the day began to break in, all the little doves began to awake and they all began to fly east to Mrs. Dove, being very hungry and thirsty. As Mrs. Dove saw them coming, she began to lay aside for them something to eat.

The little doves ate and off they went flocking together. As they flocked by the river in the noon day and as their feet were in the sand, they began to rest, the water from the river waved on the land, causing their feet then to be in mud but thy fretted not.

All the doves in one instance flew toward the river, dipped their feet in the water and up they went into the sky off to the country side where it was of much quietness and nap, nap, nap they went. Only to awaken to eat, drink and flock the more before the sun set, and the darkness set in.

UNDER THE WINGS OF MISTER DOVE TEACHER'S MANUAL

By

Pastor J.L. Moore

Chapter One

Activity/Work Sheet

THE BLACK RAVEN

Name one negative out of chapter one:________________________

Question: What was the little doves' problem that they were forced to deal with?

____

Answer: The action of the black raven.

Name three positive things out of this chapter.

1. ____________________________
2. ____________________________
3. ____________________________

Answer 1. The doves did not try to solve this problem themselves.

2. They didn't try to fight back with the raven.

3. They didn't let the action of the raven stop them.

Summary: It shows us that there will be trouble around us and we don't have to involve ourselves in it, to risk ourselves getting hurt. It also shows us that when we forgive someone for their bad actions, they can change their bad actions to good actions. It shows us that with the help of someone over us, things can change for the better. Trust in your leaders, they have the "know how" to make things better.

Chapter Two

Activity/Work Sheet

THE HUGE WORM

Name one negative out of chapter two:______________________________

Question: What enemy confronted the doves on the feeding ground?

____

Answer: The huge worm.

Name three positive things out of this chapter.

1. ________________________________
2. ________________________________
3. ________________________________

Answer 1. With togetherness, they were looking for food.

2. They shared with each other, none claimed the world to be his own.

3. In the end they were filled.

BONUS ANSWER: The worm shrunk

Summary: This chapter shows us togetherness, sharing and caring. That great things can happen when we fellowship together, sharing and caring. Great things will automatically happen to us.

Chapter Three

Activity/Work Sheet

THE HEAVY RAIN

Name one negative out of chapter three:______________________________

Question: What kind of danger were the doves in?

____

Answer: The approaching of a big storm and that they would be caught in it.

Name three positive things out of this chapter.

1. ______________________________________

2. ______________________________________

3. ______________________________________

Answer 1. They were warned about the bad weather.

2. They acted on their warning.

3. They were not disobedient to their warning.

Summary: Despite the bad weather that was coming their way. It didn't change the way they whispered to each other. By acting on the warning, it saved the little doves' lives. The little doves showed good judgment when they acted on the warning. They had good communication with Mister Dove and they trusted his decision. Therefore, when someone warns us to leave because they see danger coming, it's good to listen to them and go the opposite way, whether it's mother, father, sister, brother, friend, or teacher.

Chapter Four

Activity/Work Sheet

THE WANDERED DOVE

Name one negative out of chapter four:______________________________

Question: How did the little dove leave the shield and protection of Mister Dove?

____

Answer: He wandered away from his group.

Name three positive things out of this chapter.

1. ____________________________________

2. ____________________________________

3. ____________________________________

Answer 1. The other doves showing care for the dove even though he wandered away.

2.The other doves stayed in unity, in a group.

3.They all went to look for the dove that wandered away.

Summary: All the doves were in unity, in a group, until one decided to wander away, he became separate from the others and was not able to return on his own. Wherefore, when we have unity among ourselves, it is not good to pull away from it because by the dove wandering off, it caused the others to worry when they all could have stayed together in peace. The greatest of all is that they didn't hold it against the dove that separated because they took him to be cared for. When we care about someone, we want what's best for them regardless of what they do. At the end the little doves were all able to flock together. So if we apply this to our lives, we too can laugh together.

Chapter Five

Activity/Work Sheet

THE HUGE ANT

Name one negative out of chapter five:______________________________

Question: Why was this feeding ground unsafe for the little doves?

____

Answer: The ant had a big appetite for doves.

Name three positive things out of this chapter.

1. ______________________________

2. ______________________________

3. ______________________________

Answer 1. The little doves were caring for nothing.

2. They were not afraid when they saw the ant.

3. They left the presence of the ant and his big appetite.

Summary: This chapter shows kindness of Mister Dove to call the little doves away from the ant. Yet, he let the ant continue to find his food. Truly the little doves were in danger of the ant. It shows us that by the ant wanting to do harm to the doves, he was left alone to find his own food when it could have been that the doves would have given him something to eat. Therefore, when we do bad things or want to do them, we sometimes might end up having to live bad.

Chapter Six

Activity/Work Sheet

NOISES IN THE NIGHT

Name one negative out of chapter six:______________________________

Question: Why were the little doves' sleep interrupted?

____

Answer: The doves being frightened, awakened out of their sleep by loud noises.

Name three positive things out of this chapter.

1. ____________________________________
2. ____________________________________
3. ____________________________________

Answer 1. They had a night light as they were sleeping.

2. There was someone present to comfort them through the loud noises, to give them understanding of what was happening.

3. They were able to fall asleep again being not afraid.

Summary: This chapter shows that loud sounds can frighten us. We can be amazed when we don't have understanding. This shows us that it's a very good thing to have someone present to help us through bad times. By the doves having a restful night, they were able to get a fresh start the next morning. Furthermore, it's good to ask for understanding when we don't understand something, Truth always make us feel better.

ACKNOWLEDGEMENT

Mister Dove, my invisible friend, my immortal friend, my shield and guide. As well as my protector who became my leader and my teacher, the Lord God Almighty whom I place all my trust.

I, Pastor J.L. Moore, would like to thank the many saints for the obedience in doing the will of God in the works of Christ's Full Gospel Church of Deliverance. I would also like to thank our promoter of this book and their work in CFG.

Holy, Holy, Holy and The busy little Sheep

Pastor J.L. Moore
P.O. Box 4385
Meridian, MS 39304
(601) 482-8921
e-mail cfgc@bellsouth.net

HOLY HOLY HOLY AND THE BUSY LITTLE SHEEP

By
Pastor J.L. Moore

In the great state of Mississippi, there lived this busy little sheep. Her sheep skin was very fine and soft as feathers. Therefore, this busy little sheep was so busy that when it came time for her to eat and sleep, the good shepherd of the sheep had to say a very special word.

Even to get this very busy little sheep attention, the good shepherd of the sheep had to say that very special word.

This busy little sheep liked to play a whole lot, therefore, that is why she was called the busy little sheep.

The very special word that the good shepherd had to speak to get the busy little sheep to answer, was the busy little sheep favorite word, “Holy, Holy, Holy.

Wherefore, all the other little sheep knew her because of the favorite word the busy little sheep liked to say.

No other sheep could make that same sound, as to saying the word Holy, Holy, Holy. Nor was any of the other little sheep as busy as she was.

Seeing that this busy little sheep liked to play a lot, it took her favorite word to get her to pay attention and to slow down; Holy, Holy, Holy.

Being that this was a very special busy little sheep, therefore it took a very special word to get this very busy little sheep to respond; Holy, Holy, Holy.

One day this very busy little sheep was moving from place to place, in and out, over and under, just saying Holy, Holy, Holy.

The good shepherd of the busy little began to say Holy, Holy, Holy, and the busy little sheep would stop whatever she was doing and listen to the sound of her favorite word.

This busy little sheep that liked to play a lot, also liked to play with the other sheep. So much that the busy little sheep would not slow down to eat or sleep.

So one day the busy little sheep was outside playing with the other sheep and it became time for the busy little sheep to eat, but she would not stop playing.

The good shepherd called and called, but the busy little sheep did not hear him call.

Then the good shepherd remembered that the little sheep was a very special little sheep, and how it took a very special word to get her to stop playing, and to eat.

It was her favorite word; Holy, Holy, Holy. So the good shepherd of the busy little sheep began to say the word Holy, Holy, Holy. The busy little sheep finally stopped, and listened.

Off into the arms of the good shepherd went the very busy little sheep, and she began to eat and eat.

The next day the busy little sheep was outside playing with the other little sheep, and the time came for the busy little sheep to take a nap.

The good shepherd of this special little sheep began calling, and calling the busy little but the little sheep did not respond to the calling of the good shepherd.

Soon the good shepherd realized that the busy little sheep did not come, and remembered her favorite word. So quickly he began to say the busy little sheep favorite word, Holy, Holy, Holy.

The busy little sheep stopped, looked, and listened. The sound of her favorite word led her to the feet of the good shepherd, and there the busy little sheep went off to sleep.

The next day the busy little sheep was playing with the other little sheep, and they were playing a very special game. And the good shepherd of the sheep wanted the little sheep, he had something very special he wanted to share with her, and the other little sheep her friends.

But, as the good shepherd called he could not get the busy little sheep attention. Finally he realized that he had to say that special word to get her attention, Holy, Holy, Holy.

Quickly, he began to say them and the busy little sheep stopped playing, and listened. So off she went following the sound of her favorite word.

As the busy little sheep followed the sound of her favorite word, she began to say them, Holy, Holy, Holy. She said her favorite word all the way to the good shepherd.

All of the other little sheep followed, and they all ended up at the feet of the good shepherd. There the good shepherd had for them some very special wheat, corn, and water.

They all ate and drank with much happiness, and after they ate and drank they fell asleep at the feet of the good shepherd.

Holy, Holy, Holy; is the Lord God Almighty.

Mr. Dove, The little Girl and the Rock

Pastor J.L. Moore
P.O. Box 4385
Meridian, MS 39304

MR. DOVE, THE LITTLE GIRL, AND THE ROCK
By
Pastor J.L. Moore

This is a story about a little girl that could not make any friends so she began to live a life of sadness, and of tears.

During the summer months the little girl would go outside to sit upon this particular rock until she became very close to this rock.

During the night she would look out her bedroom window to check on the rock, and afterward she would go back to bed. One particular day in the month of July and it was very hot and the sun was beaming,

although it didn't stop the little girl from going outside to sit upon her friend the rock that called her friend. On this particular day she took along some company with her, a glass of sweet lemonade and as the little girl was sitting upon the rock drinking her lemonade, she began to cry and the tears would fall from her eyes into the lemonade and onto the rock.

The sun was beaming as the little girl sat crying, she cried so much upon that rock until her dress began to get wet, and she noticed her dress being wet, she went inside to change clothes and did not return back to her friend Mr. Rock.

The following day the little girl went outside being sad as usual to visit her friend the rock, she took with her a tall glass of water. As she was sitting on the rock with her head down, tears begin to fall from her eyes

There was so many tear drops that they caused a small mud puddle beside her and as she decided to go back inside, she stepped down into the puddle and her little white shoes were covered with mud.

The little girl went into the house to change shoes and laid down on her bed to read a book, she read until darkness came and afterward she getting up to check on her friend the rock, and found it to be in place she then began to get ready for bed. She put on her favorite gown and off to sleep she went.

When the little girl awaken the next morning her gown was all wet, she had cried during the night. The following evening the little girl went outside to visit her friend the rock, on this day she did not take anything with her.

As she was sitting on the rock she began to cry, then a voice spoke. Little girly why cry this day? The little girl looked and looked but didn't see no one from where the voice came, the voice spoke again,

LITTLE GIRL, WHY CRY THIS DAY!!!

The little girl looked again but could not see from where the voice came or who was speaking. So the rock said it is I, your friend Mr. Rock that is speaking to you. Answer me, WHY CRY YOU THIS DAY? The little girl could not answer her friend, and she didn't know exactly why she cried.

The rock spoke, Cry no more, I am your friend. I will be here always whether it rain, snow, or whether the sun is shining or the wind is blowing. From the month of January to December, I'll be right here. The little girl began to feel comforted, knowing she had a friend that she could talk to and the friend would talk back with her. So the little girl returning back to her home just-a-skipping. As night came she prepared for bed and so she did.

The next day about noon the sun was shining bright and the little girl could hardly wait to visit her friend. As she was sitting upon the rock she spoke, Hello friend! The friend replied Hello! As she was sitting she began to cry, and at this point the rock stop talking and her tears which were so many began to float her and the rock away, the little girl began to be frightened.

When suddenly she looked up toward the sun and quickly her tears was all dried up. She and her friend stop floating and she began to smile and to laugh also her friend joined in with her, she picked the rock up and took him back to his spot where he said he'll always be.

Though the little girl sat in the sun, it never got a chance to shine on her face because she always had it down. When she decided to look up, the sun shined on her and dried up her tears. The little girl had made herself two friends that cared for her so much that they caused good to happen to her. So the little girl, the rock, and the sun became close friends. She could hardly wait until summer for the sun to shine, thought she visited her friend the rock often as she could. Most important she knew her friend the rock was always there when she needed him.

During the winter months she could see him through her bedroom window, and when it rain likewise. When it snow just like her friend said, he'll always be there for her. The little girl didn't have regular friends like the boys and girls because she always washed them away with her tears until she found someone that would be her friend no matter what, it's good to make friend but in making friends you have to be joyous.

When you are joyous it causes you to make friends, sadness and tears keep friends away. So when school began the little girl that was known for sadness and many tears was seen smiling and laughing, and many came up to greet her and to befriend her. Thanks to her friends Mr. Rock and Mr. Sun. The little girl had a wonderful school year throughout, and she remained smiling and laughing and lived that way thereafter.

GOD LOVES HIS CHILDREN

Up to 4 years of age.

GOD LOVES HIS CHILDREN

Name: ____________________

Lesson 1

Directions:

OPEN YOUR BOOK TO GENESIS.

LOOK AT VERSE 1.

Teacher help each child.

1. COLOR THE WORD HEAVEN, AND COLOR THE EARTH.

1. GOD MADE HEAVEN AND EARTH.

2. WHAT DID GOD MAKE? ________________________

3. COLOR THE WATER AND LAND.

4. Teacher is to read to children.

"GOD MADE HEAVEN AND EARTH IN ONE DAY."

5. WHAT DID GOD DO IN ONE DAY?______________________________

Lesson 2

GOD MADE DAY.

1. COLOR THE DAY.

2. WHO MADE DAY?________________

Lesson 2

GOD MADE THE SEAS

1. COLOR THE SEA, THE BOAT, AND THE LIGHTHOUSE.

2. GOD MADE THE BOAT AND THE LIGHTHOUSE, THEN WHO MADE THE SEAS?____________________

Lesson 3

1. COLOR THE GARDEN THAT GOD BROUGHT.

GOD BROUGHT FOOD

2. GOD BROUGHT WHAT?_______________________

Lesson 3

GOD GAVE US A YARD

1. COLOR THE YARD

2. WE HAVE GRASS IN WHAT?________________________

3. WE PICK UP PAPER, STICKS, AND NEWSPAPER FROM OUR YARD.

Lesson 3

GOD BROUGHT A CROSS TO SAVE US

1. COLOR THE CROSS

2. WHAT IS THE CROSS?________________________

3. WHO DIED ON THE CROSS?___________________

4. HOW MANY PEOPLE HE LOVES?_______________

5. HOW MANY PEOPLES DO YOU LOVE?_______________

6. WHO LOVES MORE PEOPLES?_____________________

7. NOW THAT YOU KNOW, WILL YOU LOVE THE SAME AS JESUS DOES?________________

Lesson 4

GOD MADE LAND AND WATER

GOD MADE FISHES AND ETC…

GOD MADE BIRDS & ANIMALS

GOD MADE A ZOO

1. COLOR THE LAND AND WATER CREATURES THAT GOD MADE.

2. GOD MADE THE FISHES, THE ZOO, AND MANY OTHER ANIMALS
   CAN YOU NAME THE ONE WE MISSED?____________________

3. DOES IT LIVE ON LAND OR WATER?____________________

4. WHAT LIVES IN THE WATER?____________________

5. WE GO TO THE ZOO TO SEE WHAT?____________________

6. NAME ALL THE THINGS GOD MADE THAT YOU SEE, AND COUNT THEM.

____

____

____

____

7. NAME THE THINGS GOD DID NOT MAKE.

____

____

Lesson 5

GOD GAVE US FARM ANIMALS

1. COLOR THE FARM AND THE ANIMALS.

2. NAME THE SMALL ANIMALS THAT GOD HAS PLACED ON THIS FARM?

____

3. WHO GAVE US THIS FARM?_______________________

4. HE WHO GAVE US THIS FARM HAS A SON, WHAT IS HIS NAME?__________

5. WHERE IS THIS SON?___________________

Lesson 6

Review Over past Lessons:

All is to repeat.

> "GOD MADE HEAVEN AND EARTH, DAY AND NIGHT, WATER AND LAND, FOOD AND FARM ANIMALS, AND MANY CREATURES."

1. WHO MADE MANY THINGS?______________________________

2. STAND AND NAME SOME OF THEM?____________, ____________, ____________, ____________

3. DID GOD GIVE US ANY BIRDS, COWS, CANDY, OR CROSS? ____________

4. TELL US SOMETHING ABOUT THE CROSS, AND WHY?______ AND ________________________.

5. WHO IS JESUS CHRIST?__________________________

6. WHAT IS HIS FATHER'S NAME?__________________________

7. WHERE DOES HE LIVE?_______________________________

A. NAME THREE THINGS GOD DID NOT MAKE? 1.______________, 2. ______________, 3.______________

B. WHO LOVES EVERYBODY?_____________________________

C. WHO MADE THE HEAVEN?____________________________

D. WHO MADE THE EARTH?____________________________

E. WHO BROUGHT US THE FARMS?______________________

F. WHO MADE THE SEAS?_____________________________

1. DO YOU LOVE EVERYBODY?________________________

2. WHAT BOOK OF THE BIBLE DID YOU OPEN UP TO VERSE ONE?__________

3. WHAT DID IT SAY GOD MADE?___________________________

4. HOW MANY DAYS DID IT TAKE GOD TO MAKE HEAVEN AND EARTH?______________

5. NOW THAT WE KNOW JESUS LOVES US, SHALL WE LOVE OTHERS?__________________

COLOR THE THINGS THAT GOD MADE.

Lesson 8

1. COLOR THE PEOPLES THAT GOD MADE.

2. WHO MADE MAN?____________________

3. WHO MADE WOMAN?_________________

4. WHO DID GOD MAKE FIRST?_____________

5. WHO MADE US?_______________________

JESUS SAVES US FROM SIN

5-7 Years of Age

FROM SINS

"LIVING AS A CHILD of GOD"

Name______________________________

Lesson 1

WHO IS JESUS?

Reading-have each person to read, while they wait for the teacher to draw and color a picture on the next page that shows Jesus with children around him.

JESUS IS SAVIOR, HE WAS A BABY IN BETHLEHEM

HE HELPED PEOPLE, AND DIED ON THE CROSS TO

SAVE US FROM SINS. AND I SHALL LEARN THE THINGS

JESUS DID FOR ME.

1. JESUS IS OUR________________________________?
2. HE WAS A___________________________________?
3. HE DIED ON A ______________________________?
4. TO SAVE US ________________________________?

Teacher please go over this with the class, read verse John 3:16.

Have the class to write out John 3:16.

Jesus is God's son, that we may live forever.

1. WHO IS GOD'S SON_________________________________?

2. HE WILL GIVE US ____________________________________?

(draw a picture)

Use a extra sheet of paper to draw the picture.

Teacher is to read this story to the class.

God had sent his son down to the earth, so that we may live as God do. Meaning, so we can live a holy and righteous life. To be good, and to do as we are told by our parents. Some bad people took Jesus and put him on a cross, Jesus stayed on the cross until he had died and soldiers came and wrapped him and put his body in the tomb, It's like a cave. (draw a spiritual picture).

But on the third day Jesus rose up by the spirit, His blood saved us from sins, so we do not have to die.

(draw an angel)

1. What is this story about ____________________________________?

Teacher please read the story over until the class understand)

Teacher have the class to read aloud.

JESUS SAVES PEOPLES, AND
JESUS SAVE ME.

3. CAN ANYONE SAY, WHERE DID JESUS GO ____________?
(Heaven)

Lesson 3…cont

WHO IS THE BAD MAN?

Teacher read:

When you do bad things, you are to be punish, Not only because you did it but to teach you that it is wrong.

DID YOU KNOW JESUS WAS TEMPTED ______________________?

1. WHO KNOWS WHAT TEMPTED MEAN? (SAY ALOUD)
   1a. IT'S SOMETHING THAT'S BAD THAT YOU WANTS TO DO.

LET'S LOOK

DRAW A GIRL LOOKING AT A CAKE ON THE TABLE

CAKE

TABLE

Lesson 3 cont

YOU SEE A CAKE ON THE TABLE. AND YOUR MOTHER TOLD YOU NOT TO TOUCH IT. BUT YOU LOOK AND YOUR MIND TELLS YOU, YOU CAN'T WAIT. WHAT DO YOU DO ____?

ANSWER: YOU DON'T TOUCH IT CAUSE IT WILL CAUSE YOU TROUBLE.

(DRAW A LINE BETWEEN THE GIRL AND THE CAKE)

THIS LINE IS A WALL, SO WHEN YOU CAN'T SEE IT, YOU DON'T WANT THE CAKE.

WELL, JESUS WAS TEMPTED A LITTLE DIFFERENT BY A BAD SPIRIT, CALLED SATAN. IF ONE OF YOUR FRIENDS TELL YOU TO JUMP OFF A HOUSE, WILL YOU? NO, WELL SATAN IS A BAD MAN THAT TOOK JESUS ON A HIGH BUILDING AND TOLD HIM TO JUMP OFF, AND HIS ANGELS WOULD CATCH HIM.

(draw a picture that mention this)

WELL JESUS TOLD SATAN "IT IS WRITTEN THOU SHALL NOT TEMPT THE LORD THY GOD."

Meaning, He IS CASTING SATAN AWAY FROM HIM.

Lesson 3…cont

NOW YOU SAY ALOUD, IT IS WRITTEN, IN THE NAME OF JESUS CHRIST.

Again, IT IS WRITTEN, IN THE NAME OF JESUS CHRIST.
Again, IT IS WRITTEN, IN THE NAME OF JESUS CHRIST.

NOW, SAY IT TO YOURSELF IN YOUR HEART THREE TIMES, WHEN YOU ARE DONE RAISE YOUR HAND.

DO YOU KNOW WHEN YOU ARE TO USE THIS CASTING? (have them to write the answer)

____

____

WHEN YOUR MOM OR DAD TELLS YOU NOT TO DO SOMETHING, AND YOU ARE GOING TO DO IT, STOP AND SAY, “IT IS WRITTEN, IN THE NAME OF JESUS CHRIST.” AND TURN AROUND AND GO AWAY FROM IT.

DO YOU KNOW WHY YOU ARE SAYING THIS?________________

ANSWER: TO KEEP FROM GETTING INTO TROUBLE.

JUST LIKE JESUS SAID IT, AND WHO LEFT?__________________
(satan)

Lesson 4

HOW TO BE GOOD AS A CHILD OF GOD

1. YOU SAY, IT IS WRITTEN WHEN YOU WANT TO STOP FROM DOING SOMETHING WRONG.

2. DISCUSS ALOUD WAYS OF BEING GOOD.

3. DRAW A PICTURE OF SOMETHING GOOD.

4. COLOR THE BIBLE, AND THE CROSS.

JESUS TEACHES US A STORY

Teacher turn to, MATTHEW 18:1-4.

1. WHO DO YOU BELIEVE IS THE GREATEST IN HEAVEN _________?

LET'S SEE, LISTEN TO THIS STORY.

PEOPLE WHO HAVE HEARD THE WORDS OF THE BIBLE. MEANING, HAVE READ THE BIBLE OR HAVE WENT TO CHURCH, THEY WILL LIVE IN HEAVEN WITH GOD.

YOU AS CHILDREN WILL TRAIN OR CAN TRAIN YOURSELF TO BE GOOD, AND A KIND PERSON. AND WITH THESE LESSON YOU WILL BE ABLE TO UNDERSTAND THE BIBLE, SO IF YOU ARE GOOD AND HAVE GOD'S WORDS IN YOU, YOU SHALL HAVE FAITH IN GOD.

Lesson 5…cont

1a. WHAT IS FAITH______________________________________?

IT'S WHEN YOU BELIEVE IN GOD, AND JESUS, AND WHEN YOU LOVE THE LORD.

LET US SING THIS SONG.

JESUS TEACHES ME HIS LOVE,

HOW TO LOVE THE LORD WITH

THE FAITH I HAVE IN ME,

MY FAITH FOREVER GROW.

Teacher: sing the song three times or until they remember it. Every Sunday it is done.

So IF YOU DON'T HAVE GOD, THEN WHO ARE YOU__________?

YOU BECOME A SINNER, A MEAN PERSON LIKE SATAN, YOU ARE BAD AND SELFISH, AND YOU DON NOT LIKE TO SHARE.

COLOR THE PICTURE (draw a spiritual picture)

Let's Learn To Use The Bible

New Testament:

1. OPEN YOUR BIBLE TO MATTHEW

2. LOOK ON THE PAGE FOR THESE LETTERS "MATTHEW" KEEP TURNING.

3. YOU MAY GET THE TEACHER'S HELP.

4. TURN TO CHAPTER 2

5. TO FIND CHAPTER 2, LOOK FOR THE BIG NUMBER 2 AT THE TOP OF THE PAGE.

EXAMPLE PAGE

6. TO FIND A VERSE IN CHAPTER 2, YOU LOOK AT THE LITTLE NUMBERS. FIND VERSE 3

7. MATTHEW IS A BOOK OF THE BIBLE, CHAPTER 2 IS THE BIG NUMBER IN THE BOOK OF MATTHEW. VERSE 3 IS THE LITTLE NUMBER IN CHAPTER TWO IN THE BOOK OF MATTHEW.

NOW FIND LUKE

NOW FIND THE BIG NUMBER 2.

NOW FIND THE LITTLE NUMBER 14.

LOOK AT THE WORD AND CHAPTER, THEN THE VERSE, TRY AND WRITE A VERSE.

WRITE AND THEN FIND MARK 3:2

MARK IS THE BOOK

3 IS THE CHAPTER
2 IS THE VERSE

* help will be needed.

THE COLON (:) IS USE TO KEEP THE CHAPTER AND VERSE APART.

LOOK UP THESE

LUKE 1:2

JOHN 2:5

WHEN YOU ARE DONE AND YOUR TEACHER HAS SEEN IT, COLOR THE BIBLE.

1. THE CHAPTER NUMBER IS ______________________________.
2. THE VERSE NUMBER IS ________________________________.

TO FIND A BOOK OF THE BIBLE MATCH THE SPELLING OR WORD.

1. MARK.	A. LUKE
2. JOHN.	B. MARK
3. LUKE.	C. JOHN.

Lesson 6…cont

JOHN MARK JOHN

LESSON 7

WHAT DO YOU DO TO BE SAVE?

BELIEVE IN GOD, JESUS, AND HIS HEAVEN ABOVE.

THE BIBLE IS LIFE, MEANING IT IS USE TO FEED THE SPIRIT.

Opening out:

YOUR HEART IS GOOD AND CLEAN.

NOW, YOU BROKE MOM DISH OR GOT A BAD GRADE, YOURS HEART IS BROKEN AND SAD. SO YOU READ THE BIBLE AND IT MAKES YOU HAPPY, SO YOUR HEART IS BACK GOOD AND CLEAN.

YOU WILL FEEL GOOD INSIDE. WHEN YOU ARE HUNGRY, YOU ASK YOUR MOM TO FIX YOU SOME FOOD.

WHEN YOUR HEART IS BROKEN, THEN YOU ASK MOM TO READ TO YOU ABOUT JESUS.

LISTEN TO THE STORY BELOW.

JACK'S MOM BAKE A CAKE WITH FROSTING ON TOP, SO JACK CAME IN AND SAW THE CAKE ON THE TABLE. HE SAID, "IT IS WRITTEN IN THE NAME OF JESUS CHRIST" AND HE LEFT. BUT JACK HAD A BAD DAY AT SCHOOL, KIDS ALWAYS CALLED HIM NAMES, AND HE WANTED TO CALL THEM NAMES. BUT IS THAT RIGHT? NO, SO JACK SAT AT THE TABLE AND HIS MOM GAVE HIM A PIECE IF CAKE, AND A CUP OF MILK.

HE WAS FULL AFTER THE SNACK, BUT HIS HEART WAS BROKEN DOWN AND SAD, SO JACK'S MOM CAME TO HIM AND READ HIM A STORY ABOUT HOW PEOPLE TALKED ABOUT JESUS, BUT HE FORGIVE THEM. SO JACK SAID TO HIMSELF, IT IS WRITEN IN THE NAME OF JESUS CHIRST, AND HE COULD GO TO SCHOOL AND WOULD NEVER BE WORRYED ABOUT KIDS WHO TALKED ABOUT HIM.

Lesson 7…cont

DO YOU KNOW WHY ________________CAUSE HE HAD FAITH IN GOD

1. WHEN SOMEONE TALKES ABOUT YOU, WHAT DO YOU SAY____

____

____

____

COLOR:
(draw a spiritual picture)

LESSON 8

WRITE OR TELL WHAT YOU HAVE LEARNED FROM THIS LESSON BOOK.

Lesson 8…cont

COLOR:

(draw a spiritual picture)

Lesson 8…cont

COLOR:

(draw a spiritual picture)

COLOR:

(draw a spiritual picture)

Lesson 8…cont

MATCH THESE TOGETHER

MARK. .MARK

LUKE. .JOHN

JOHN. .LUKE

Mr. Dove and The Three Talking Chickens

Pastor J.L. Moore
P.O. Box 4385
Meridian, MS 39304
(601) 482-8921

MR. DOVE AND THE THREE TALKING CHICKENS

By
Pastor J.L. Moore

Let me tell you of about the story of three talking chickens that lived in a coupe and was very unique as they could be, each with a talent of their own. They liked to share their talent among each other. One of the chickens was called Harry, and he was the fattest of the three, he had feathers as the color of brown and he had eyes as sharp as a eagle, and he could see afar, far and wide.

This is what made him so unique, he knew of many things by color; red, blue, green, brown, yellow, black, violet, tan, and many other colors. He also knew a many different sizes and shapes, and the things he could see afar he would share it with the other two chickens.

He would tell them about the many different colors that they could see and described it, and many different sizes he could recognize by shape, and all would laugh and talk about the things Harry told them which made them grow closer to each other.

The other chicken was called Tom, he had a very unique talent also he could hear very good, so much as hearing a straw of hay falling to the floor. His talent took him deep into the world where he could hear sounds that was not familiar to him and the others, sounds of children swinging and children laughing, people talking, and the sounds of the wind.

The things Tom heard, he would share it with the other two chickens, and they asked questions about the things he could hear deep into the earth.

This is how they were able to teach each other the things they were not able to know or learn on their own.

The third chicken was called Cindy, she was the smallest of the three, she had a talent that was unique as well. She could smell high and low, far and near. She could even smell the wind and its different odors. Fruits, peaches, oranges, and bread.

Even their favorite food like corn, and odors of flavors; grape strawberry, and lime. Odors of sweet and bitter. She too would share with the other two chickens the things she learned from her talent, and not to long all were seeing afar, hearing and smelling afar.

They thanked each other and called each other friend. Therefore, daily life in the coupe became very special in a way it never was before. By opening up to each other they became close friends and very smart.

WORK SHEET

The summary of Tom; Though he is small and fragile his talent is the biggest of himself, he glow with excitement being able to do something so fantastic and above all to learn and share with other.

1. What makes Tom so special ______________________________

____?

2. What does he do with his talent____________________________

____?

The summary of Harry; Though he is the quiet of them all, by discovering his talent he could not help but speak of the things he was able to recognize variation in sounds words by letters.

1. Was Harry afraid to share his talent__________________________

____?

2. What were some of the sounds he heard______________________

____

____?

The summary of Cindy; Her uniqueness enabled her to explore different smells, and she was sensitive to the five food groups as well as other things of the earth.

1. What group is she sensitive to_____________________________

____?

2. How many food groups are there___________________________

____?

3. Can you name the food groups that Cindy smelled______________

____?

WORK SHEET

On the following work sheets describe some of the things that Harry seen, by drawing them in the blanks.

1. shapes

a: ______________________________

b: ______________________________

c: ______________________________

d: ______________________________

Mister Dove, The Great Light, and Mr. Owl

Pastor J.L. Moore
P.O. Box 4385
Meridian, MS 39304
e-mail cfgc@bellsouth.net

MISTER DOVE, THE GREAT LIGHT, AND MR. OWL

By
Pastor J.L. Moore

The Great Light that shines all the time, as it shines it reveals. All the people were astonished at this Light except for one person, Mr. Owl. Because this Light was so bright Mr. Owl was not able to do the things he liked to do.

Mr. Owl was afraid of the light because of its continuous shining Mr. Owl had to keep his eyes closed. So he would go in his cave that he called his home.

The Light was so great that it even shines in the cave of Mr. Owl who loved the darkness because it gave him a chance to do the things he liked to do.

Mr. Owl loved to have his way all the time, because the Light was so great it began to cut out a lot of Mr. Owl's favorite games. Mr. Owl liked to play ugly games with the people, he would cause their belongings to disappear.

Mr. Owl became so ugly inside with his games that he began to cause many people to become sick. As these people began to be sick and their possessions began to disappear they began to be very afraid.

Until one day an angel appeared to one of the people to whom the owl had made ill, the angel told the woman that there was only one thing that could make their troubles go away, and the woman answered, who?

The angel spoke, all you have to do is call the Great Light. As she began to say, "Oh Great Light." "Oh Great Light." This Great Light shined brightly on her.

At that instance she began to feel very good and strong. All of her possessions began to be restored. The Great Light made the woman healthy and her possessions unbreakable.

The Great Light knew who was the cause of the woman's trouble and all the people knew that Mr. Owl loved darkness and liked to play games with the people.

So this woman wanted this Great Light to shine on Mr. Owl, so the woman asked the Great Light to shine on Mr. Owl and the Great Light was happy to do so and it did.

When the Great Light shined on Mr. Owl, all of the owl's inside was revealed, many of the peoples belongings was inside of Mr. Owl and there was this bug inside of him also. The Great Light spoke to the woman, it is not Mr. Owl that likes to play games with the people that cause them to be sick or their belongings to disappear.

It is the bug that is in Mr. Owl. He made Mr. Owl do the things he did. It was because Mr. Owl loved darkness so much that this bug was able to get inside of Mr. Owl.

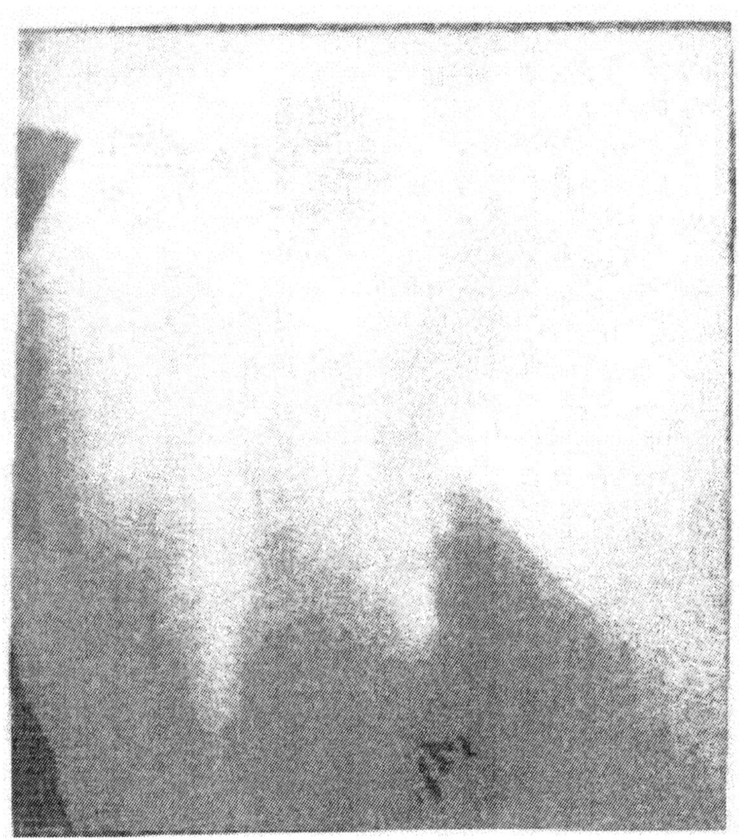

Then the woman spoke, "take the bug out of Mr. Owl Oh Great Light," and her request was granted. The bug disappeared, the people belongings and Mr. Owl began to love the Great Light until one day Mr. Owl was able to open his eyes to the Great Light and it did not hurt him at all. Then Mr. Owl shouted, "I'm free, I'm free" and off he flew very happy. All were happy.

The Great Light…The Lord God Almighty.

www.ingramcontent.com/pod-product-compliance
Ingram Content Group UK Ltd.
Pitfield, Milton Keynes, MK11 3LW, UK
UKHW040559210726
13854UKWH00008B/1587